I WROTE THESE

A COLLECTION

OF

POETRY AND PROSE

D. K. MAMULA

All rights reserved. All material within these pages is original to the author and may not be reproduced or used in any manner whatsoever without the express written permission of the publisher.

ISBN-10: 0-9966515-3-5
ISBN-13: 978-0-9966515-3-0

© Copyright 2016 by D. K. Mamula

I have been writing for years. Poems, essays, stories, diaries—my writings came in many forms and ranged from complete fiction to complete truth. As I grew, my writing became more personal and I began writing more about my thoughts and feelings. High school and college courses helped me to write more creatively and exposed me to different styles.

I loved reading books and the library was—and still is—one of my favorite places. It was like being in an unending buffet, all of it free for the taking, and I couldn't get enough. There were books on every possible subject and I was able to explore those shelves of books to my heart's content. The stories I read were thrilling, scary, funny, heart-breaking and heart-warming. True or fictional, I was influenced in some way by all of them.

I began to notice that I had a flare for words, and by the time I was out of school, I had amassed quite a collection of original work. I'll admit, it wasn't all good. As a matter of fact, some of it was downright corny. I have kept just about everything I have ever written, the majority of which has never been read by anyone except me. That, however, is about to change.

In this book, you will find several pieces of my original work that span at least four decades of my life. They include poems and writings of different lengths covering a wide range of subjects. Most of this material expresses the way I was feeling at the time it was written and those feelings are evident in the words used to compose the piece. Some may find my words harsh or even a bit offensive, but I will not apologize for them. The truth of what I felt would not have been conveyed properly otherwise.

The thoughts, views and opinions expressed here are completely my own and are in no way meant to refer to any particular person, group or circumstance. I do hope, however, that the words you are about to read inspire you, move you and, at the very least, make you pause for a few moments and consider in greater detail the world we live in and the people with whom we share it.

All the best…

D.K.M.

With The Turn of a Page

A page turns, a chapter ends
What has been will never be again

Close the door, turn the key
What has always been will forever be

We can't go back, we cannot change
The past cannot be rearranged

The whistle has blown; the game has been played
Our lifetimes lived, our memories made

A page turns, a chapter begins
The future starts where the past ends.

The Piano

It's a lonely sight.

That beautiful white piano there on the stage.

It seems to long for someone to play just a few more songs...

        for someone to make the show go on for just a little while longer.

It longs for gentle fingers to caress the keys with a beautiful melody...

        or for strong hands to pound out the rhythm of the city streets.

It has so much to say to us with its exquisite melodies...

                so many emotions to share...

But alas, there it stands... alone...

        surrounded by its own infinite beauty.

That lovely white piano on that empty, desolate stage...

              Waiting for the show to go on...

The person I am now is a composite of the life I have lived so far... this one moment in time does not define me.

I have always believed that respect has to be earned, but I'm starting to rethink that opinion.

If people seem to always let you down, there are three possible reasons and three possible solutions:

1. Your expectations are too high; lower them.

2. Your expectations are unrealistic; change them.

3. You're expecting imperfect beings to be perfect, according to your standards; don't.

BE FREE

Let yourself be free as the wind and you can fly over the sea in a loving kind of way. Over mountains and trees, just floating in the breeze, like a leaf floating to the ground.

MY HEART NEEDS YOUR LOVE

My heart needs your love to hold, cherish, and keep forever. Throughout life. Throughout happiness and sorrow. Then, when your love dies, and I no longer have you to help me stay alive, I shall find another heart... another love... another you. And I shall start over again, needing your love to hold, cherish, and keep forever. Throughout life. Throughout happiness and sorrow. Throughout eternity.

BECAUSE I DREAM

When life gets tough and it seems as if there's no other way out, I start to dream.

I like to dream.

In my dreams, I can imagine how the future will be. I can make my life go in the direction I wish it to go.

If I wish it to be happy, I can make it happy and if I wish it to be sad or tragic, I can make it go in that direction. I can make it happy and then suddenly tragic or I can make it tragic and then suddenly make it happy.

But whatever direction I lead my life and however happy or however tragic I make my dreams, I know that in my real life anything is possible. The more I dream, the better prepared it makes me feel for the real-life happiness and tragedy that my real life has to bring.

So life, I'm ready for you.

Not only because I live, but because I dream, too.

I Met an Angel

I met an angel years ago—never thought I would
And every time I said "I can't", she whispered that I could

When I stumbled, she helped me stand, she caught my tears when I cried
It seemed no matter where I went, I could feel her by my side

She gave me the right words to say when things needed to be said
She gave me pause to stop and think when angry thoughts filled my head

She guided me in each decision and helped me choose right from wrong
And I felt her hold my trembling hand at times when I wasn't so strong

She filled me with unselfish desires each time I bowed my head
And kept a steadfast and faithful watch as I slept in my bed

She remains my strength and courage, inspires me to this very day
She resides now deep within my heart where she will always stay

WHAT IS PEACE?

Peace.

What is peace?

Is it something we must fight and kill mankind to find?

Or does it come from brotherly love?

Must the people of the world give their lives so others can find peace?

Someday mankind will find peace, but I'm afraid there won't be anyone around to enjoy it.

I ask again, what is this thing we call peace?

What is it like?

And will we ever find it?

If you are waiting for others to validate you, it's going to be a long wait. I suggest you bring a good book and find a comfortable seat.

You can tell a lot about a man by the way he wears his socks.

If you're doing something for someone with the expectation of getting something in return—even a few words of gratitude—you're doing it for the wrong reason.

WHEN THE ROSE BLOOMS

When the rose blooms in Spring
It's such a beautiful thing
But when the rose dies in Fall
Then there's nothing left at all

And when spring comes
The rose blooms again
And as sure as the rose
We'll be together my friend

Try not to be afraid
Of the promises you've made
Just keep pushing on
Try to be gentle, try to be strong

Smile when the world grows dim
And dream of places you've never been
Don't let your heart be darkened by the bad
And don't be ashamed to cry when you're sad

We'll all become what we're meant to be
For we were all born with a certain destiny
Sooner or later I'm sure we'll all see
That it's okay to be just you and me

So continue to plan the future
And dream on my friend
For we'll be together soon
When the rose blooms again

Remembering Mom...

"Oh my God! I've turned into my mother!"

We've heard that phrase a million times, and we think of it as a terrible thing. What really confuses me, though, is why it's looked upon as such a curse.

When I was a child, I would watch my mother as she cleaned the house, cooked dinner, paid the bills, did the shopping, and in between all that handled any crisis that came along without complaining. It didn't matter what it was--husband, kids, relatives, car trouble, house trouble, money trouble--she dealt with it.

Her family was always top priority. She worked hard to do her part in her marriage. If her children needed something, she didn't mind sacrificing to get it for them. Brothers and sisters, cousins, nieces and nephews, in-laws--it didn't matter, family was family. If she could help, she would. If someone was sick or a family member had passed, she was there. If the phone rang, she always had time to talk. She would laugh with you or cry with you, whatever the moment brought. Even if her heart was breaking, she would put on a strong front for her family. I can't remember a day in our lives together that she didn't tell us that she loved us.

I remember being able to ask her anything. We talked about everything. She told me her memories of her childhood, of friends long lost and mistakes made. She had few regrets and she didn't speak of them often, but the few she had were meaningful to her.

I remember how she was able to laugh at herself--some of my favorite memories of her were times like these. I remember falling over in fits of laughter with her over something as simple as calling the phone company or trying to find her glasses.

I remember how easily she made friends, and how long she kept them. She always had someone she could call if she really needed help, and always had someone outside the family she could confide in.

I remember how our friends used to call her "Mrs. D". They were always welcome in our house. She was a mentor to them, and a couple of them who had some hard times with their own parents told her that they wished she had been their mom. She put up with all of our craziness, but didn't take any of our crap. She always let us know when we were stepping over the line.

I remember how she always took pride in the way she looked and how she presented herself. I used to watch her as she did her hair and make-up. She would always comment that she wished her hair was thicker or that her teeth were better looking or how she needed to lose a few pounds, but I always thought she was the most beautiful woman in the world.

She was strong, warm, loving, kind, gentle, compassionate, dependable, graceful, talented, artistic, charming, and loyal. She was a shoulder to cry on, a hand to hold, and a friend to rely on. She was the first to stand up for what was right, and she wasn't afraid to admit it if she was wrong. Everyone who knew her respected her, whether they liked her or not, she made sure of that. She loved her family, her country and God. A smile or a hug was always returned without any thought, and love was always given unconditionally.

I'm older now, and when I look at my reflection in the mirror, I see my mother's eyes and my mother's smile. When I speak, I hear her in my words. When I am feeling playful, I hear her laughter, and when I am angry, I feel her strength. When I see my family, I feel the pride she felt when she looked at us. No matter what I do, I try to do my best and take pride in it, just like she did. When I think of my little baby grandson, I can now understand how she felt when she was waiting for my son to be born, and how she just couldn't wait to hold him in her arms. Even as I type this, I look at the keyboard and see my mother's hands.

She was more than my mother. She was my mentor, my guide, my protector, my teacher, my nurse, my confidant... she was my hero... and now that she's in Heaven, she's my Guardian Angel.

Yes, I am my mother's daughter. But it didn't happen suddenly, she's been there all along. I don't think of it as a bad thing, but rather a blessing. There's no one else I would rather be like than her.

Happy Mother's Day, Mom... I Love You...

I can win half the battle just by showing up for the fight.

No one is perfect, not even you. Take the time to get to know other people--their habits, their personality, their strengths and weaknesses. Then, good or bad, you'll know exactly what to expect from them.

I don't always have to scream to get someone's attention.

Day Is Done

I come home from work

And crawl into bed

You wrap your arms around me

Nothing needs to be said

And you pull me closer and closer and closer

Until we are one

The day is done

The following poem was written for my cousin, Judy McCrobie East, as a tribute to her baby brother, George, who died as a result of wounds he sustained during the Vietnam War. It wasn't until decades later that his family learned the truth about how he died. He was mortally wounded because he threw his body over a fellow soldier to shield him from the flying debris. His family's search for the truth about what happened that day brought together many of the soldiers that served with George, and helped my cousin and her family find some much-needed closure. In the end, they learned that he was a hero. At the time of his death, Cpl. George Edward McCrobie was 20 years old.

George

I hear your voice on a soft summer breeze
As you whisper in my ear
Reminding me that you're not really gone,
That your presence is always near.

The sun shines like your brilliant smile
That always warmed my days,
The wind reminds me of your strength
You showed in so many ways.

The rose that blooms when winter snows
Cover the cold, hard ground
Brings to mind the courage you showed
When the world had you down.

As I make a wish on a shining star

That falls from the midnight skies,

I think back and remember

That playful sparkle in your eyes.

And then the rain from clouds of gray

Makes my heart relive that mournful day

When they came to tell me that you had died...

And I sat down...

                alone...

                              and I cried.

Though many loves have come and gone,

Our love is like no other,

For it shall stand the test of time,

The bond between a sister and her brother.

If you don't take yourself seriously, then you shouldn't be surprised if no one else does.

Sometimes, in order to get where I'm going, I have to take the scenic route. I can't always get there from here.

I don't always have to be right... and I'm not always wrong.

WHILE I WANDER

Sometimes, when I wander through the night by myself, I think of my life and everyone in it. Sometimes I want so much to change all the bad parts and throw away all the problems and troubles that come with life. At times I want to chase all my worries away and let the sun shine in, but I know that no matter how sweet life is there will always be bad times and there will always be problems... and troubles... and worries. And through all of the bad parts the sun will still shine no matter how gloomy life may get. I used to let the bad times in my life destroy my dreams, but no longer will I let my dreams be conquered and overcome. From now on, I will protect my dreams and when life gets bad, I'll know my dreams and I will protect each other... during the night... while I wander.

I can handle this. I just have to relax and remind myself that I've already done this once, so I know I can do it again.

Hate can make even the most beautiful people ugly.

Where I desire to go in my life isn't necessarily where I was meant to be.

Denial turns a blind eye

Insinuation hurts so deep

Vicious rumors, accusations, lies

Ominous signs that love won't last

Regrets and reminders of the past

Children caught in the middle

Everyone always loses a little

THE MOON

It is a cloudy night
But I can see the moon
Way up in the sky
Almost like high noon

Surrounded by dark clouds
It seems so gloomy and gray
I'm glad I don't always
Have to look at it this way

In and out, over and under
Through the clouds it flies
As I stand, watching the moon
Up in the cloudy skies

The Tender Red Rose

In the backyard of the house I live in, there stands a small rosebush. It sits rather close to the ground and has very few branches, but it is by no means weak or frail.

I know this, because over the past fifteen years, I have watched as it was blown by the fierce winds that broke limbs from nearby trees. I watched as it was pelted by giant raindrops during torrential spring storms. One summer, its blooms and branches were beaten down by a sudden hailstorm that spit hailstones the size of golf balls furiously out of the sky. In the winters, I have looked out to see it holding its own as freezing rain coated it with a solid sheet of ice that didn't melt for many days, or snow that piled so high it actually buried the little bush, hiding it from view for several weeks. There was even a year when it was mowed down—literally cut to the quick—leaving only a tiny stump where the bush had existed. I was sure that it was gone for good, that the roses I had looked forward to each year would never return... but they did. Every spring they budded and bloomed, just as they have always done.

When I look out and see the bright red petals of each flower spread wide to soak up the rays of sunshine, I smile. I am amazed at how something so beautiful, something so soft and tender, could be so strong and resilient. It never quits—never. It is in these ways that the little rosebush reminds me of you.

It reminds me of the strength of your spirit and how it weathered any storm with dignity and courage. It reminds me how you stood your ground through downpours of teardrops and the ever-growing pile of problems that seemed determined to bury you. I am reminded of how you braced yourself against the hailstorm of unfair judgements and icy innuendos that chilled you to the bone, and how you were strong enough to withstand the fiercest winds that everyone thought would surely uproot you... instead, you swayed with them until they passed. Your beauty shone through it all—your touch, soft and compassionate; your heart, warm and tender; the sunshine of your smile; your arms always reaching out to those in need, like the petals of the flower. It's very appropriate then, that the red rose was your favorite of them all.

For as long as I shall live, I will see you every time I look into the face of a tender red rose...

My Broken Heart

(In memory of my mother, Betty Rosalie Garrison Dillihay)

My broken heart will never heal.

It just hides behind memories until the moment you enter my thoughts again.

Then it comes out and reminds me what's missing in my life.

And then, selfishly, I cry.

A few years ago, as I listened to all the news reports about the recession and how bad things were getting and heard everyone complaining about what they had to do without, I got to thinking about all the blessings I've had in my life. I decided to make a list of all the things I am truly thankful for...

I'm Thankful

I'm thankful for the sun in my eyes

And thankful for the air in my lungs,

I'm thankful for living to be this old

And thankful for still being this young.

I'm thankful for the music in my ears

And the song that plays in my heart,

I'm thankful for being able to stop now and then

And for being able to once again start.

I'm thankful for the rain falling from the sky

And for the snowflakes that light on my face,

I'm thankful for cool breezes in the summertime

And, in winter, for a warm fireplace.

I'm thankful for the hands that allow me to touch

And for the feet that allow me to walk,

I'm thankful for aromas that tempt my nose

And the voice that allows me to talk.

I'm thankful for the chaos of life being lived

That reminds me I am alive,

I'm thankful for the moments of quiet peace

That make me glad I survived.

I'm thankful for the stars above me at night

And the ground beneath my feet,

I'm thankful for the grass that grows so green

And the flowers that smell so sweet.

I'm thankful for smiles and laughter and joy

Shared with loved ones through the years,

I'm thankful for every moment, good and bad

Even for the heartache and tears.

I'm thankful for the ocean, the waves and the shore

For the mountains, the trees and the land,

For the Earth, the sky and this great universe

God created with a wave of his hand.

I'm thankful for all the friends I have made

Whether we are near or far apart,

I'm thankful for all that my eyes can see

And for those things only seen by the heart.

I'm thankful to be living in this amazing world

And able to experience all its beauty,

I'm thankful to know I am part of it all

And to know it's all a part of me.

Where I am at any given point in my life does not dictate what I am capable of... but it does give me a hint of what ELSE I am capable of.

A person can speak without talking, hear without listening, feel without touching, see the invisible and love without expecting anything in return.

If I'm not willing to work for it, I probably don't need it.

To earn a child's love, respect and gratitude...

You **don't** have to be the best mother, the best father, the best aunt, the best uncle, the best sister, the best brother or the best grandparent.

You **don't** have to be the best coach, the best teacher, the best soccer mom, the best scout leader, the best athlete, the best stage mother or the best cheerleader.

You **don't** have to have the fanciest house or the coolest car or have the most money or buy them the best presents or throw the best birthday parties.

You **don't** have to be the strongest, the prettiest, the most educated, the most popular or the most fun.

But you **do** have to be present in their lives—in whatever way possible.

You **do** have to allow them to be the crazy, funny, messy, loud, beautiful little unstoppable balls of energy that they are, and also allow them to grow into the crazy, funny, messy, loud, beautiful, creative, unstoppable, passionate beings they were meant to be.

You **do** have to take the time to listen to them, to talk to them, to play with them, to laugh with them, to cry with them and to share your experiences with them.

You **do** have to be there to support them and, when the time comes, be able to let them stand on their own.

You **do** have to be ready to heal their boo boos and ouchies with a magical kiss, to hold their hands whenever they feel scared or lonely, to provide a place within the comfort of your arms for their broken hearts to heal.

You **do** have to say 'no' every now and then, even if they tell you they hate you for it...

But most of all, you have to love them... and make sure they know it.

Empty Storefronts

Paint peels, bricks fall

Buildings crumble as grass grows tall

Memories of what we thought would last

Quickly fade into the past

Long lost like a forgotten grave

Is there anything left to save?

Generations watch through unconcerned eyes

As our history slowly dies

Why?

Why?

Why do we insist that everyone fit into a specific mold?

Why do we try to live up to the expectations of others?

Why is it that we never feel pretty enough, tall enough, thin enough,

        smart enough, talented enough, fast enough, strong enough...

Why is it that we never feel that we are enough?

Why do we accept the opinions of people who know nothing about us?

Why is it that we never question outsider's opinions of ourselves,

        but always question our own opinions of ourselves?

How can strangers be so right about us and how can we be so wrong?

Who could possibly know more about us than ourselves?

Why do we let people treat us as though we are less than worthy?

Why do we allow their judgements of us to become our own?

Why do we not accept each other for who we are, the way we are?

Why?

Someone else's opinion of me is just that... someone else's opinion... and their opinion of me doesn't matter. The only opinion of me that I should be concerned about is the opinion of the person I see in the mirror every morning.

Fear can be a great motivator or a debilitating roadblock. It's up to me to determine which it is and what to do about it.

Just because the crazy train stops at your station, it doesn't mean you have to climb aboard!

This House, This Home

If something here looks out of place

And in the dust your name can be traced,

Keep a smile on your face

For your friendship we'll embrace

This house isn't meant to be a showplace,

This home is meant to be a living space

Zzzzzzz...

If sleep is overrated, as some people say,

Then why do I miss it so much every day?

An hour here, an hour there,

They must be adding up somewhere.

In a vault, in a safe, or maybe in a bank?

If I knew for sure, I'd rob them, to be quite frank.

You can be sexy without being sleazy
You can be naughty without being nasty
You can be racy without being raunchy
You can be glamorous without being gaudy
You can be alluring without being annoying

I have experienced better times, but I have survived worse.

I should try every day to do the best I can do to be the best I can be. That's all I can really ask of myself... and that's all I can really ask of anyone else.

Do What You Want

Do what you want to do, whatever it is.

If it makes you happy... if it fills you up... if it sets you free... then do it. Just do it.

If you want to sing, then sing. If you want to dance, then dance. If you want to paint, then paint.

If you want to cook, then cook. If you want to write, then write.

If you want to swim, if you want to plant flowers, if you want tell jokes, then do it.

If other people tell you it's a waste of time, don't believe them.

They're wrong.

It doesn't matter if other people don't approve. It doesn't matter what they think or say.

If other people don't like what you're doing, fuck 'em.

This is your passion.

Tell them to go find their own.

Satisfaction

We complain about our weight while inhaling Krispie Kremes

We complain about how we're treated while treating others mean

We complain about pollution as we toss our trash aside

We complain about the smog, but refuse to share the ride

We complain about the government, but never cast a vote

We complain about the fire after ignoring signs of smoke

We complain about education, but refuse to pay for schools

We complain about rule-breakers, but refuse to follow the rules

We complain that children are starving, but never have enough to share

We complain no one will leave us alone, then complain that no one cares

We complain about those who take advantage while taking all we can for free

And though we're friends, I complain about you and you complain about me

We live in a world of constant want and constant need

Where satisfaction is forever chased, but never guaranteed

I don't have to like everyone and it's okay if someone doesn't like me... sometimes even I don't like me.

One missed detail can completely change the outcome of any situation.

There are times in life when walking away is your best option.

The Silence

So much is happening in the silence
As our lives and those around us unfold
Things of which we'll never know
So many stories yet to be told

As we enjoy the peace and quiet
Somewhere a war rages on
As we mourn for voices now silenced
Others are raised up in song

As many lands drown in drought
Torrential rains soak other shores
As the oppressed declare they've had enough
Those with too much beg for more

And in a distant forest
A mighty tree crashes down
Does it make any noise
As it thunders to the ground?

The very sound of silence itself
Is one of the loudest you'll ever hear
It exposes all of our secrets
It intensifies all our fears

If you linger in the silence,
You should always beware
It will not hold in confidence
The secrets you leave in its care

So much is happening in the silence
As our lives and those around us unfold
Things of which we'll never know
So many stories yet to be told

Where Am I?

Where am I?
Where have I gone?
I haven't seen me
for so long.
I look in the mirror,
But the person I see
Just doesn't seem to
remind me of me.

What can I do?
I'm feeling so down.
Everything's changed now
that you're not around.
My world has gone dark,
There's nothing left in my view
Except old faded memories
of me and you.

I want to change,
I want to let go,
And the longer I hold on
It just gets harder, I know.
I need to be free
Of this anger and pain,
But when I close my eyes
I only see you again.

I'm not entirely truthful when I say I don't care what other people think of me, because sometimes I do care... for about 15 minutes... then I stop caring and move on with my life.

A lot can be said by saying nothing at all.

Although I usually don't mind doing it, I don't always have to agree to wait for others. My time is just as valuable as theirs.

Everyone's Life

There comes a time in everyone's life when they stand up and say, "ENOUGH ALREADY!". I thought I had reached that point many times, but I turned out to be wrong. I do believe I'm getting extremely close to it, though. Most of the time when someone pisses me off, I rant and rave and then get mental images of that person just as the body bag is zipped closed. Lately, I just see that last part. I'm tired of ranting and raving, nobody's listening anymore. It seems more and more that actions would speak louder than words. I'd never do it... but sometimes I wish I could. We all do. Those of us who say we don't, are lying. There are just too many annoying people in this world for me to be the only one who feels this way. I'm even strong enough to admit that sometimes the annoying person is me. But I'm also big enough to apologize for it... sometimes.

There comes a time in everyone's life when they know they have to make some major changes. They have to let go of the old people and places, and find something new to latch onto. It's one of the hardest things in life to do and most people can't. They get to a certain place in their lives and then give up. They stop fighting and pushing forward. They become stagnant, feel as if they're going in circles and getting nowhere. It's easier to stay where they are and accept that this is as good as it's ever going to get than to try to make it any better. I'm strong enough to admit that I have been one of these people. I'm happy to say that I'm growing out of it... slowly.

There comes a time in everyone's life when they have to fight for what they believe in. Most people stand back and watch as a select few do all the tough stuff. It's not until after the work is done that they stand up and try to take the credit. Some like to change their beliefs to match the current hot topics. They read the papers to see what folks are into or who or what everyone is trying to save this week, then they jump on the bandwagon. As long as it's fashionable, they're in. But as soon as the next new "great cause" comes along, they're gone. If you ask them what it is they truly believe in, though, they would be hard-pressed to give a definitive answer. It's something they never actually thought about. Sadly, I must admit to being a sheep who followed the flock blindly. But my eyes are open now and I'm starting to follow my own path... and a different flock.

There comes a time in everyone's life when they must look in the mirror and really see the person staring back at them. They need to look deep into the eyes of the person in the mirror and try to see into their own soul. They should try to see the person that everyone else sees instead of the person they pretend to be to make themselves feel important. We are all so used to putting up a front to protect ourselves that we tend to lose sight of who we really are. We get so far away from our true selves that sometimes we never find our way back again. We forget what was important to us... and sometimes, we forget the people we loved. I'm greatly troubled to admit I lost track of the person in the mirror. I'm ecstatic to have found her again... finally.

There comes a time in everyone's life when they need to stop talking and start listening. Most people just go on and on without even thinking about what they are saying. They seem to adore the sound of their own voice. Apparently they think the rest of us adore it, too. News flash: we don't. Please shut up. There are too many people in this world who are all talking at the same time. If everyone is talking, who's listening? We need to take the time to listen to the important things that are being said... and to listen to all the important things that are NOT being said. Those are the things that don't need words to be conveyed. The things that are said with the heart, not the mouth. I have, unfortunately, been one of the people who had a lot to say about things that aren't so important. Fortunately, I have learned to stop voicing my own thoughts so much and to listen not only with my ears, but also with my heart.

There comes a time in everyone's life when they have to take themselves off the pedestal they have placed themselves on and realize they are no better than anyone else. We can always have more, do more, see more, know more than the next guy. But that in no way makes us better than the next guy. We may have nicer clothes or fancier cars or bigger houses. We may be more educated or make more money. But we are not better. More fortunate... maybe. But not better. More doesn't mean better. Prettier doesn't mean better. Richer doesn't mean better. Thinner doesn't mean better. We all try to live up to the world's expectations, but none of us ever attain that standard. It's impossible. There is no such thing as perfect. If there was, then there would be no reason for living. There would be nothing to aspire to. Besides, who are we to say that someone else's life is imperfect? I wasted many years worrying about being like everyone else. I have since realized that my little imperfections make me a unique human being. I love that about myself.

If you keep going and going, but don't seem to be getting anywhere, ask yourself this one question: Where are you trying to go?

Perfection, across the board, is unattainable because everyone has their own way of defining 'perfection'.

You can't get over the hump if you don't climb the hill.

The Conformist

Ignored are the traits intrinsic to me

The world sees only what it wants to see

Judgements unreserved are given for free

Mold me, shape me, hide me, change me

Scripted spontaneity falls on deaf ears

The world hears only what it wants to hear

Nameless voices dictate who I should be

Mold me, shape me, change me, tame me

A masterpiece in a worthless frame

So high is the price of gilded fame

The world creates the image it wants to see

Mold me, shape me, change me, perfect me

Refusal meets rejection, shunned in shame

Cast out are those who won't play their game

Alone in the shadows of what used to be

Deceive me, deny me, dissect me......

Forget me.

This Body

This body
I live in this body
This body that has too much here and not enough there
I live in this body

This body
I live in this body
This body you judge as imperfect and flawed
I live in this body

This body
I live in this body
This body you think of as crippled and unable
I live in this body

This body
I live in this body
This body you call unattractive and ugly
I live in this body

This body
I live in this body
This body you see as a possession, something you own
I live in this body

This body
I live in this body
This body that serves as a battleground against disease and death
I live in this body

This body
I live in this body
This body you see as emaciated and frail
I live in this body

This body
I live in this body
This body you see as battered and bruised
I live in this body

This body
I live in this body
This body you see as weak and small
I live in this body

This body
I live in this body
This body you see as seductive and irresistible
I live in this body

This body
I live in this body
This body you see as wrinkled, weathered and worn
I live in this body

We each reside in different houses
And sit high upon our thrones
And the differences between us arouses
The urge within us to cast stones

But when locks are eased and windows opened
And kings and queens step down from their thrones
When eyes truly see and love is spoken
Houses transform into homes

So let not this body deceive you
For it only shelters the truth living inside
Remember someday it may be you
Who within its skin resides

I know my weaknesses, but when measured, my strengths outweigh them.

People who act mean or grouchy or annoyed or angered or unhappy or depressed or lonely or spiteful or pushy or hateful are the people who are the most in need of a friend, but you can't force them to accept your friendship. You have to wait for them to realize that they are not alone. Unfortunately, some of them never do.

Sometimes, when people ignore you, you should consider it a blessing and enjoy the peace and quiet.

On August 2, 2008, I stood at Ground Zero. I saw the massive empty space where the Twin Towers once stood. I saw the cross that stands near it that was made from steel beams from the World Trade Center. I asked myself the same question I'm sure a lot of people have been asking—why? But there is no justifiable answer. There is no reason for this kind of hate and anger.

Across the street from Ground Zero is a small but exquisitely beautiful church called St. Paul's. In the churchyard is a cemetery that dates back to the 1700's. There is a monument there of the stump of a 100-year-old Sycamore tree that stood in the churchyard, along with several other smaller trees. On September 11, 2001, when the towers collapsed, that tree was destroyed and the churchyard was littered with debris—papers, computer monitors, chunks of steel and glass—all covered in ashes and dust. But even though St. Paul's is barely a stone's throw from Ground Zero, the church was not harmed. Not one pane of glass in any of the windows was cracked or broken. The church later served as a sanctuary for the rescue workers and volunteers who worked day and night to find those lost in the rubble. Memorial alters still stand in the church honoring those that were lost on that fateful day. Looking at the photos of the many faces, I felt as if they were all there with us. Alongside of those altars are displays of the outpouring of generosity and brotherhood that came from all over the world. As I read the notes and letters and looked over the teddy bears and the patches from firefighters, rescue workers and law enforcement officers that were sent to New York as a means of encouragement, I realized something. In that tiny church, hope lives. If you ever think that no one cares, go to St. Paul's... you'll feel it, too.

At the time of the attacks, I didn't have much to give, but felt I needed to do something. Words have always come easy to me, and while sitting one day watching news reports on TV, I wrote this poem. At the time, with the exception of my prayers, it was all I had. It may never go any further than this, but it is dedicated to the people we lost and their families. I wrote it to remind everyone of the one thing lost on September 11, 2001, that was more important than anything else—human lives.

Words are very powerful things. Maybe helping people to remember is the best gift I could have given New York.

Maybe someday I can do more....

God Bless....

D.K.M.

IN LOVING MEMORY....

of those we love

of those who went before

of those whose lives we shared

of those we'll see no more

of those whose smiles brightened our days

of those whose laughter warmed our hearts

of those whose hands held ours tight

of those from whom we were torn apart

of those who worked beside us

of those with whom our children played

of those who we respected

of those with whom we knelt and prayed

of those who tried to help

of those whose lives they gave

of those who'll never be forgotten

of those we could not save....

The steeple of St. Paul's stands tall between the cranes

Cross made of steel beams from the World Trade Center

St. Paul's Churchyard at the rear of the church.

St. Paul's churchyard—Ground Zero in the background

Stump of the 100-year-old Sycamore tree

Inside St. Paul's Church

The Memorial Altar

Some photos of the missing...

Teddy bears from children around the world

Items left as memorials on the churchyard fence

Items commonly found on the pews during the relief effort

Patches from rescue workers around the world

Tell Them

There may come a day when you wish you had said
All those words that kept echoing in your head
But time after time day turned into night
You kept putting it off, the time just wasn't right
It's okay, it'll keep, another time, another day
And all the while time was slipping away
So busy with life, both they and you
Never had time to tell them, just assumed they knew
Words never spoken, feelings never shared
Just a wave as you leave... do they know that you care?
Tell them you love them, tell them you care
Tell them you're thankful that they've always been there
Don't make them wonder, don't make them wait
Tell them now, before it's too late

My mother passed on May 22, 1992. Later that year, I met the man who is now my husband. During our first five or six years together, we moved several times for various reasons and had made the decision to store some of our belongings at my in-laws house in an effort to cut down on the number of boxes that had to be transported from place to place.

As the years flew by, I forgot about the stored boxes. For over 20 years, they sat waiting to be rediscovered. With the recent passing of my father-in-law, I was now faced with the daunting task of sifting through these many possessions.

I decided one night that I was ready, so I sat down in the middle of the bedroom floor with a few plastic bags and began going through the boxes and bags that I knew were mine. Each of those boxes contained items from my past—some high school memorabilia, several items from my son's childhood—but the majority of them contained clothes and many personal items that belonged to my mom. It didn't take long for my emotions to get the best of me.

A couple days later, I wrote the following about that experience...

I told myself it would be easier now, that they're just old clothes and it was time to let them go and let someone who really needs them use them, but I was wrong. It wasn't easy. It was one of the most difficult things I've ever done. The moment I opened that first box, you took over. Your face, your smile, your dancing eyes, your infectious laugh... all of it came rushing back, filling me with immense love and crushing heartbreak. Twenty-four years have come and gone, but it makes no difference. You were there, every memory racing through my mind like a movie in fast forward. Every emotion, every laugh, every tear was as fresh in my mind as it was when it first occurred. Sitting alone on the floor of that empty bedroom, surrounded by you, I gave in and let my tears fall.

The worst thing you can do is to deny your own truth.

Happiness is not a material object that you acquire through great wealth or a prize that you win in a lottery or a buried treasure that you have to search many years to find... happiness is not a destination that you travel to or a gift that the 'right' person will give you if you're lucky enough to find him or her... happiness is not a reward for living the 'right' kind of life or for doing great deeds or for enduring great sacrifices. Happiness is a state of being; it's a choice that anyone can make for themselves at any point in their lives. I am happy because I choose to be... it's as simple as that.

www.ingramcontent.com/pod-product-compliance
Lightning Source LLC
Chambersburg PA
CBHW060725030426
42337CB00017B/3012